IMAGES 2

The Ultimate Coloring Experience
by Roger Burrows

RUNNING PRESS
PHILADELPHIA · LONDON

Dedicated to Katy, Nigel, Cameron, and Nicholas

Printed in China

9 8 7 6 5 4 3 2 1
Digit on the right indicates the number of this printing

ISBN 978-0-7624-3909-6

Cover design by Frances J Soo Ping Chow
Typography: Clarendon and Helvetica

Running Press Book Publishers
2300 Chestnut Street
Philadelphia, PA 19103-4371

Visit us on the web!
www.runningpress.com

Welcome to this second, "jumbo edition," of *Images* designs. These are designs to color that have been created to stimulate your imagination. The designs in this book are a new group of designs gathered from earlier editions of Images books.

Hidden within each design is an infinite number of pictures, forms, patterns, animals, flowers, and more. As you color, new images will pop out and beg to be explored. Use colored pencils, markers, or crayons to unlock your creative potential!

Have you ever seen something out of the corner of your eye—and just for a moment, not understood what it was? Have you ever looked at cracks on a wall, or clouds in the sky, and seen images of things—just like seeing elephants in the clouds? All of these things give you a clue as to how ideas form in your mind.

The younger you are, the less likely you will be to over interpret something that you see. A baby will look at an object and not be able to interpret it—they might be looking at a teddy bear from an "odd" angle, and not "recognize" it. Just turn a teddy bear around before a very young baby—and you'll see their delight when they can recognize it for what it is. A child will look at a few lines drawn on a sheet of paper and "see" many things—one changing into another. An adult, if they see anything at all, will tend to see one thing—and they'll fixate upon it. Ideas are the same. For a young child, almost anything is possible, and believable. As a child matures you can often see the flexibility of their imagination melt away.

When you look at these designs let your imagination roam—and you'll find that *Images'* designs will seem to change in front of your eyes. When an image does form, don't fixate upon it, let it go, and see what else "pops-up" into your visual imagination! As much as you can let your imagination roam you can also deliberately look for things! Can you find a bird, or a flower, for example? If you deliberately "look" for specific things you'll start to combine your "visual logic" with your visual imagination. Whatever image you do find you'll be able to find it repeated again and again in other parts of the design. You'll be able to find the image the same way up, reflected, and rotated.

For the mathematically minded imagers, the designs are based on different systems. You'll find that most of the designs are based on close packing circles, but you'll also find designs based on other systems. All the designs are derived from precise geometrical relationships, so explore the symmetries and try to find the unit cell that is repeated: rotated, reflected, and translated. Try to figure out the principles used and see if you can build the equations that underlie the designs. There are no "casual," lines; every line has mathematically calculated position.

Hope you enjoy this book!

Can you find the elephants in the design to the right? Remember that, whatever shapes or picture you find, you can find them again and again—rotated and reflected.

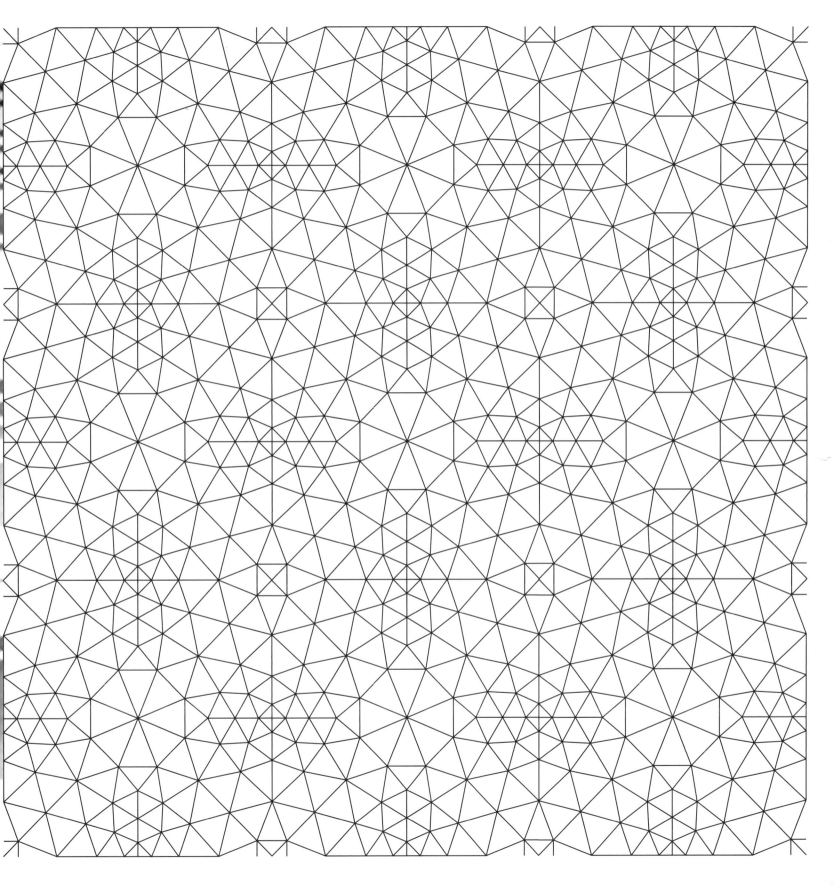

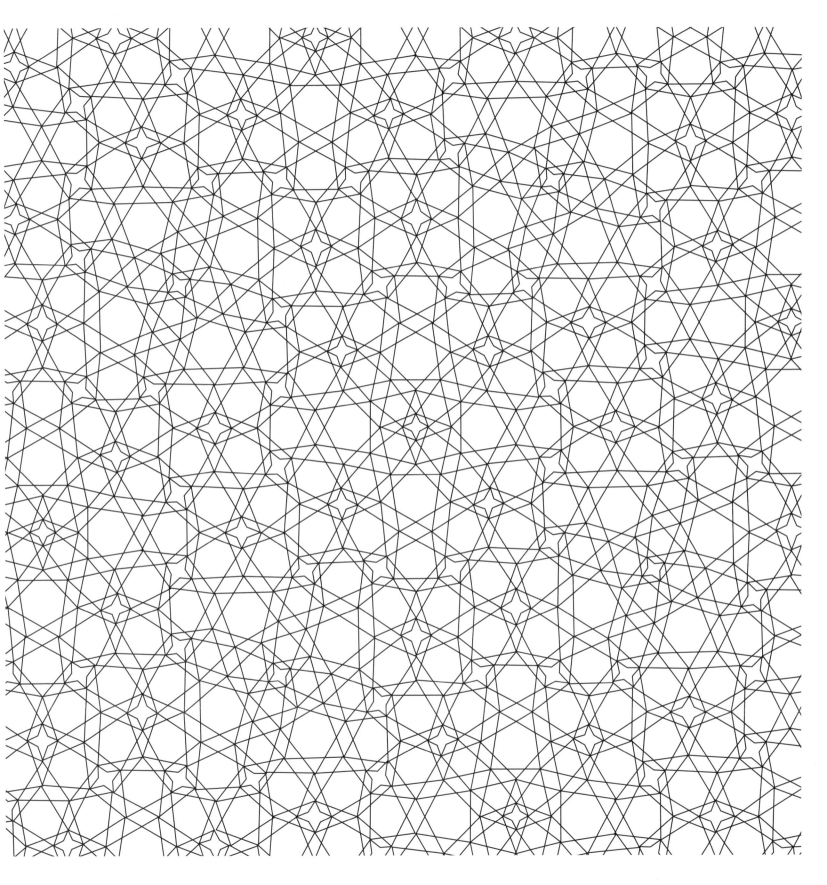

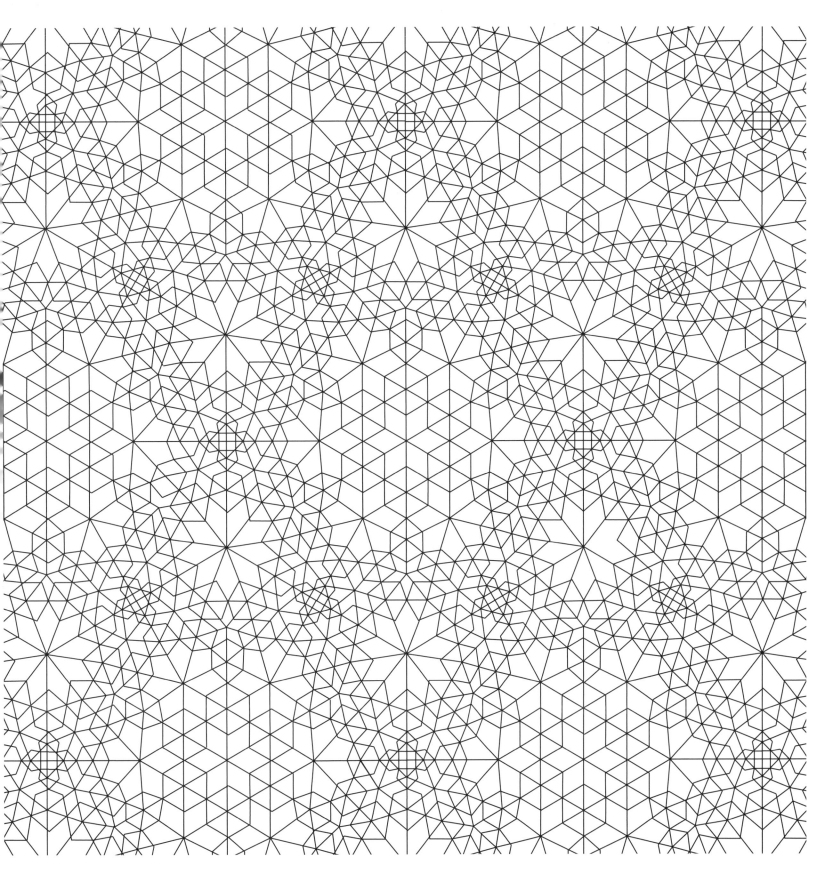

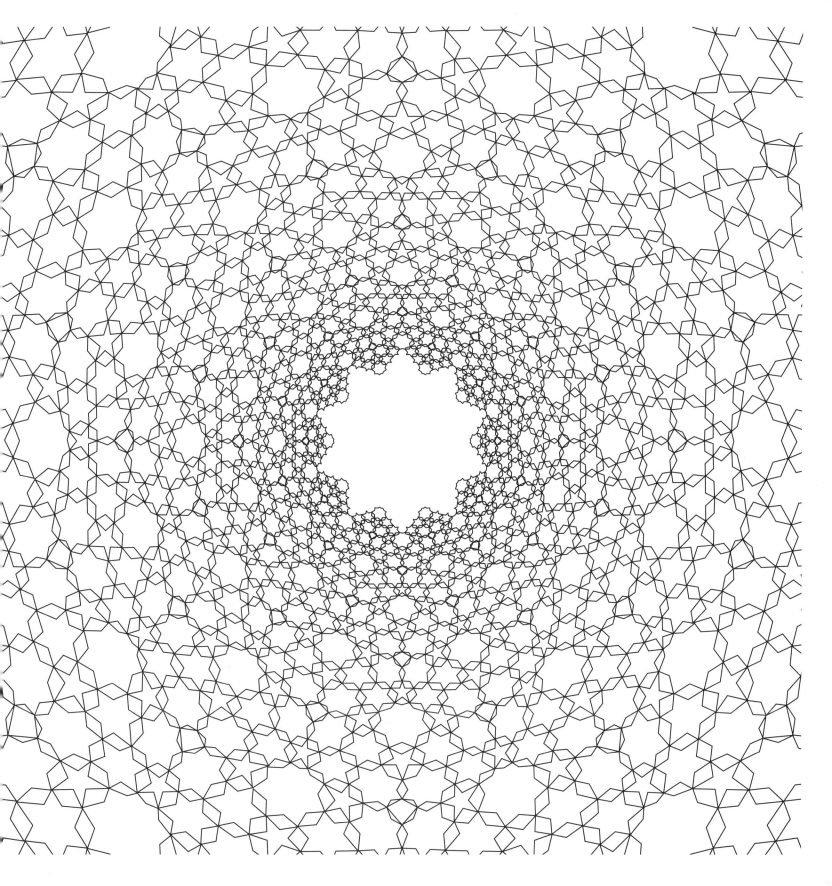

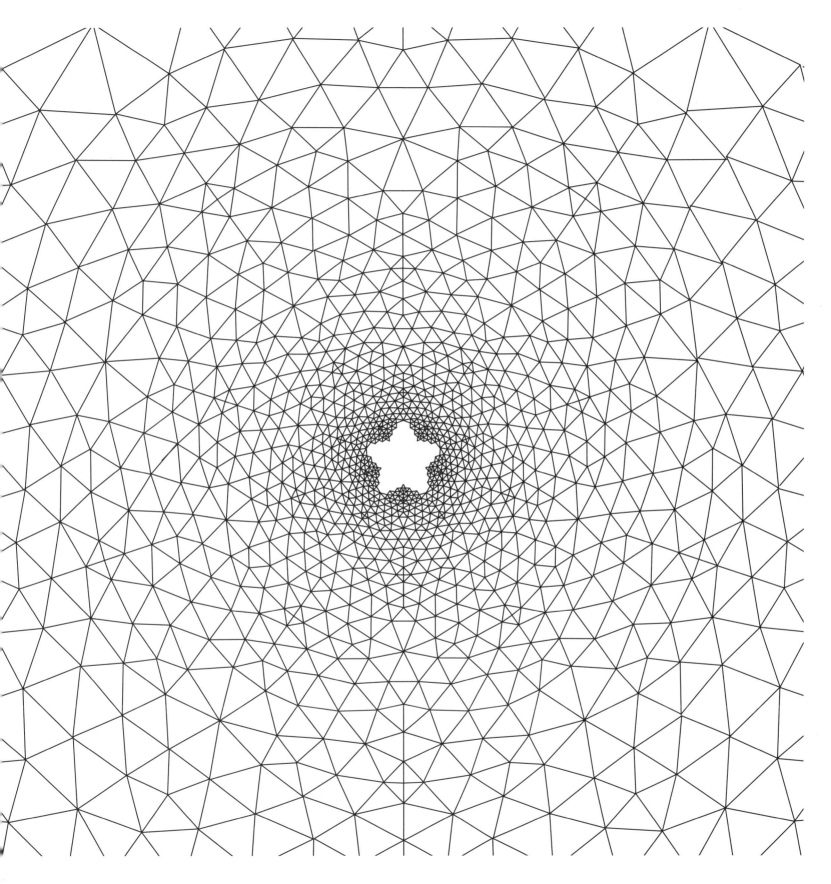

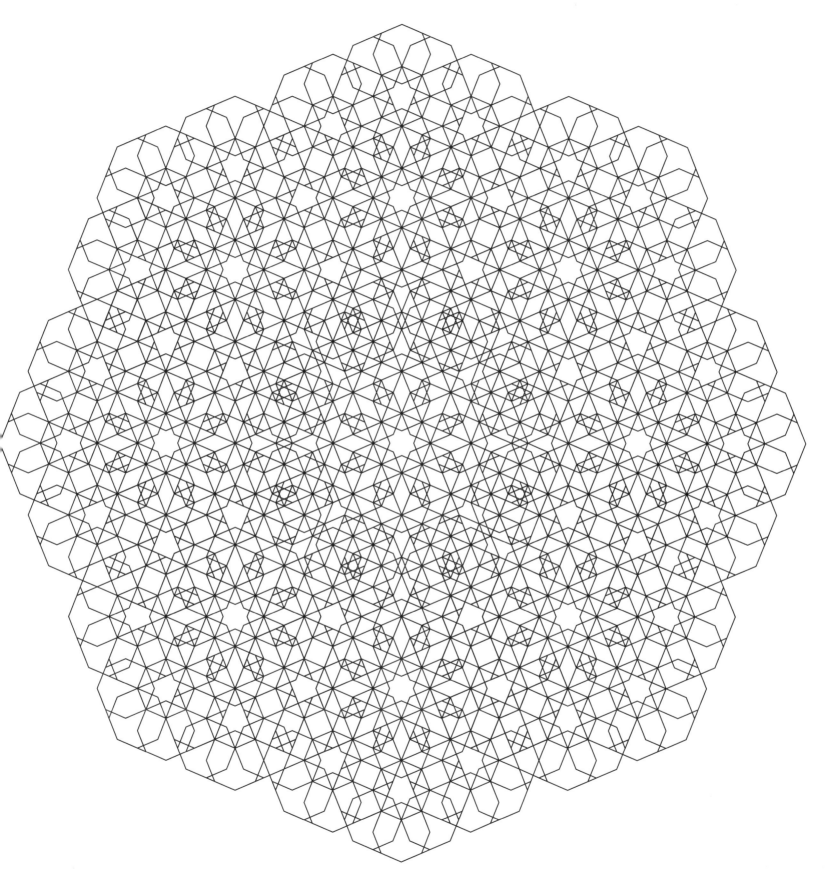

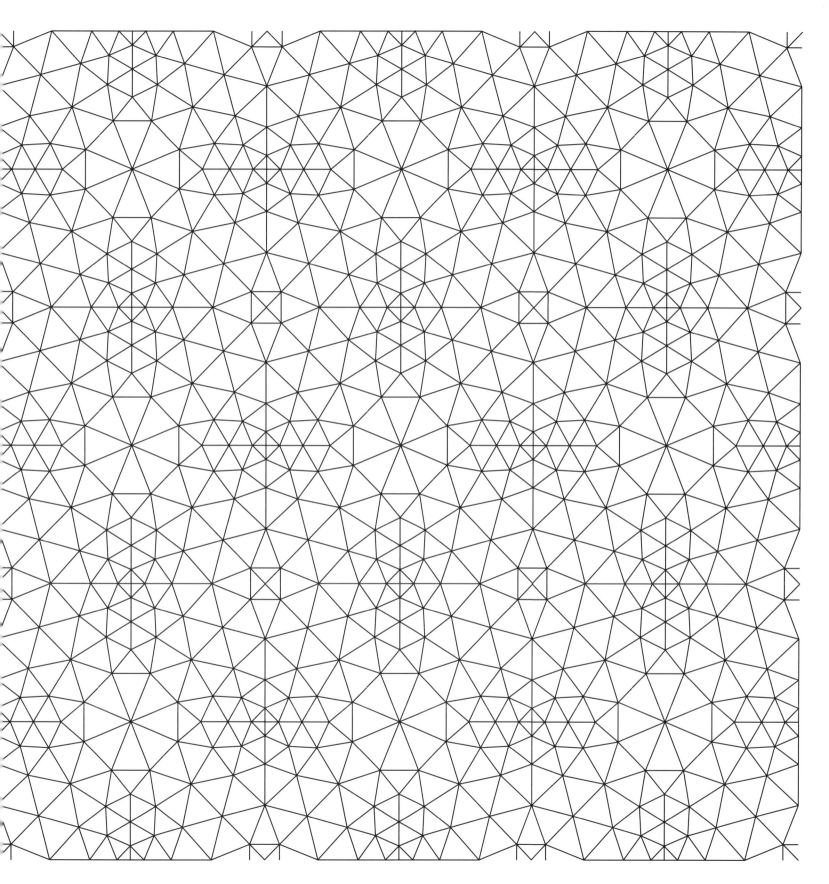

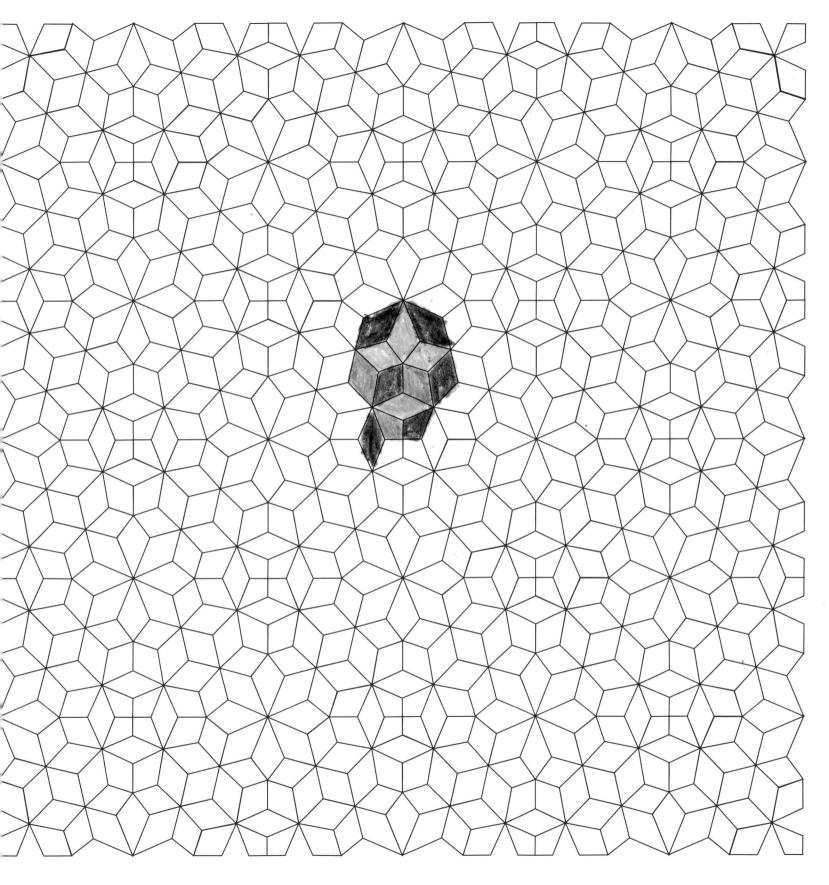

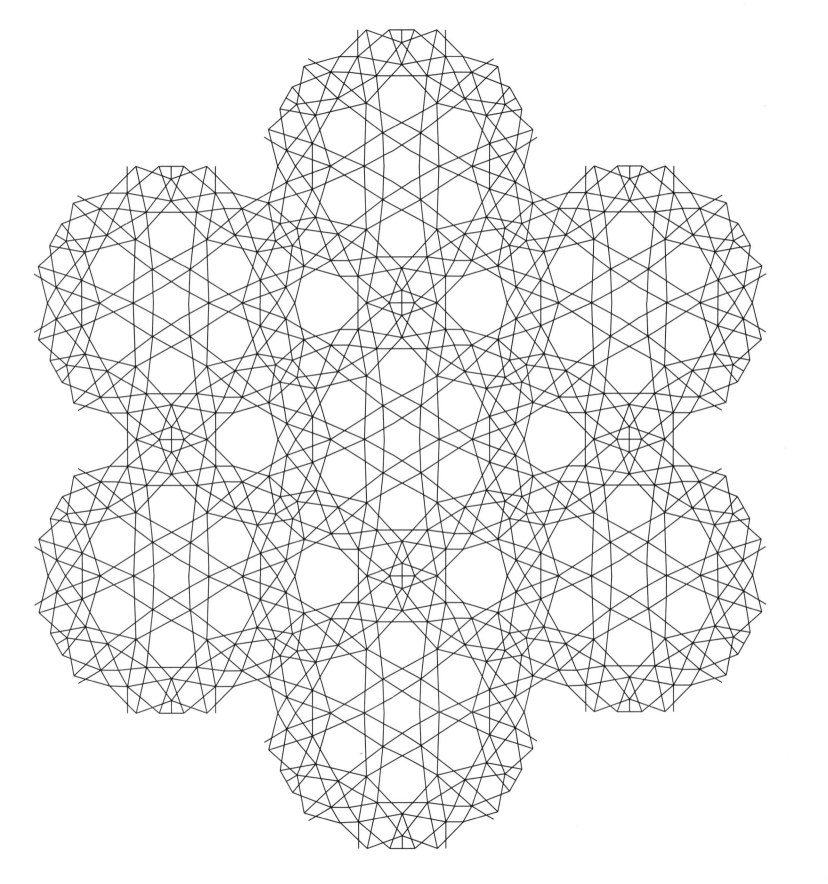

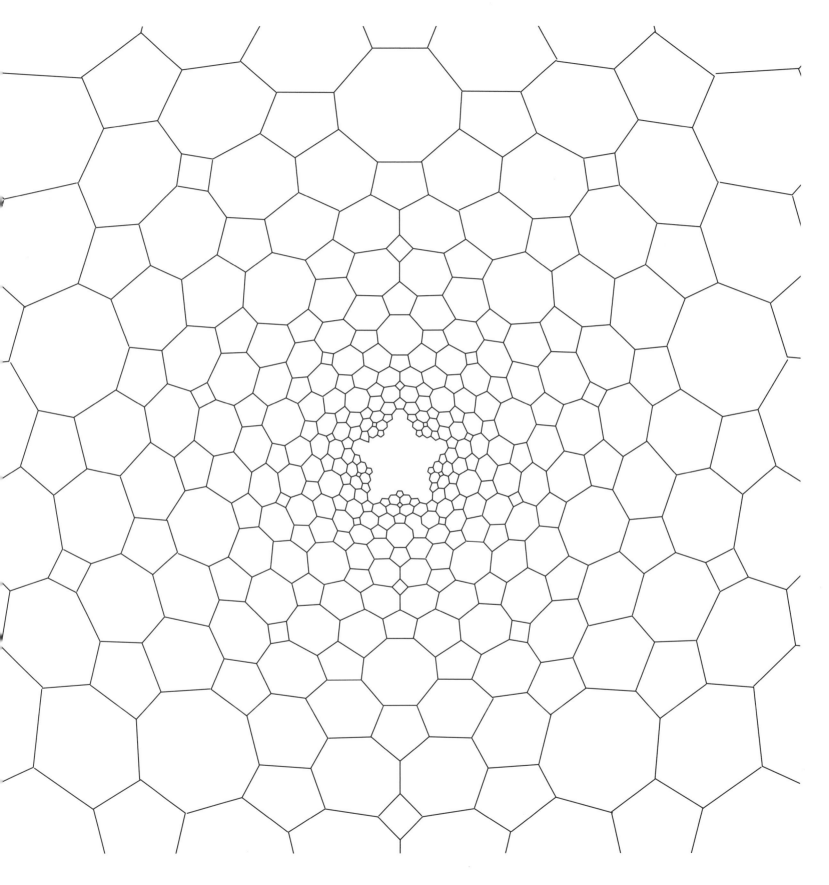

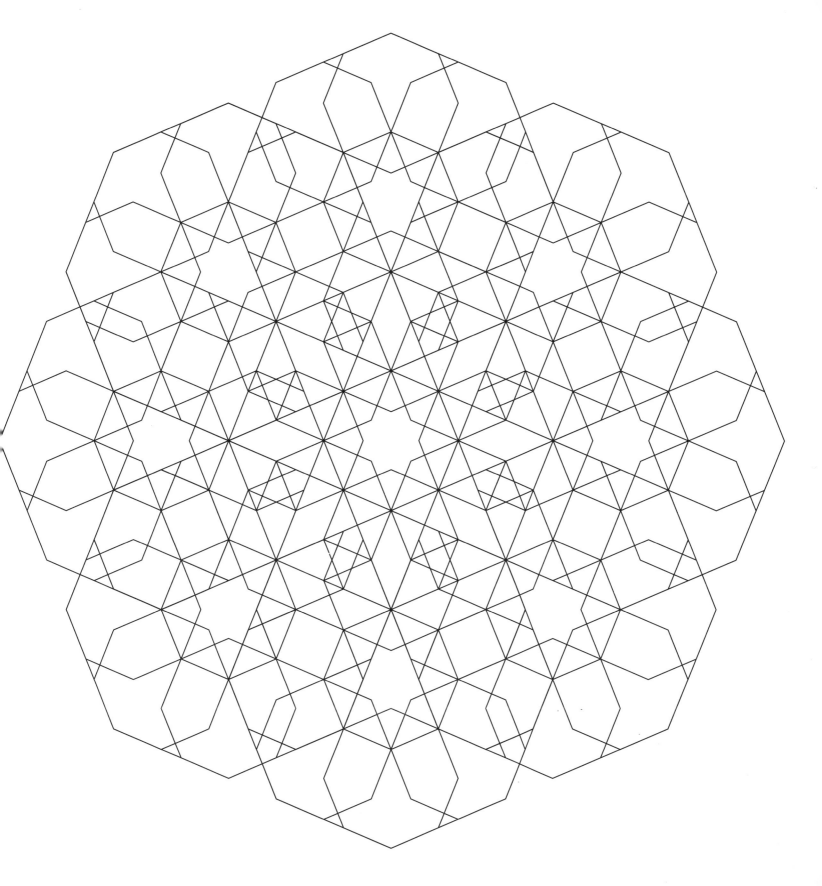

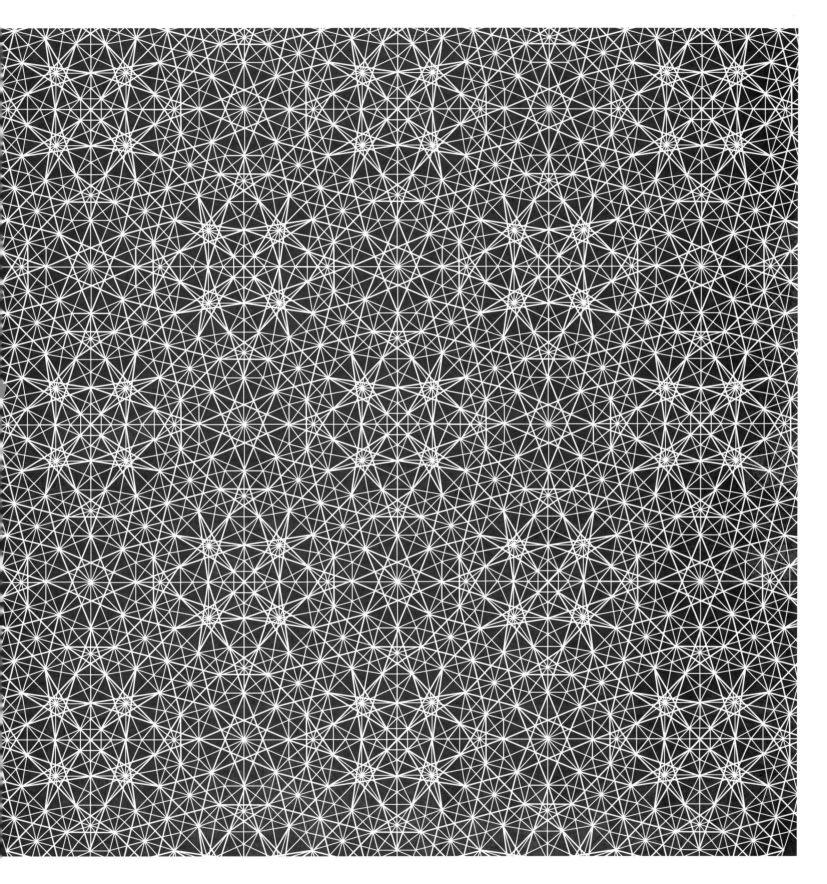

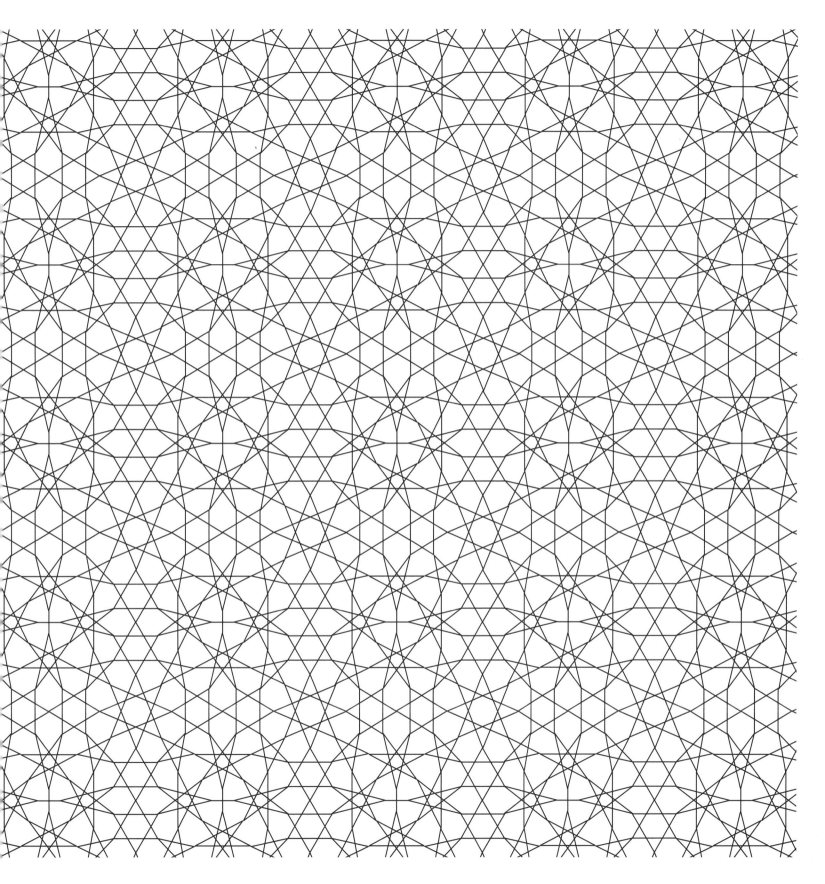

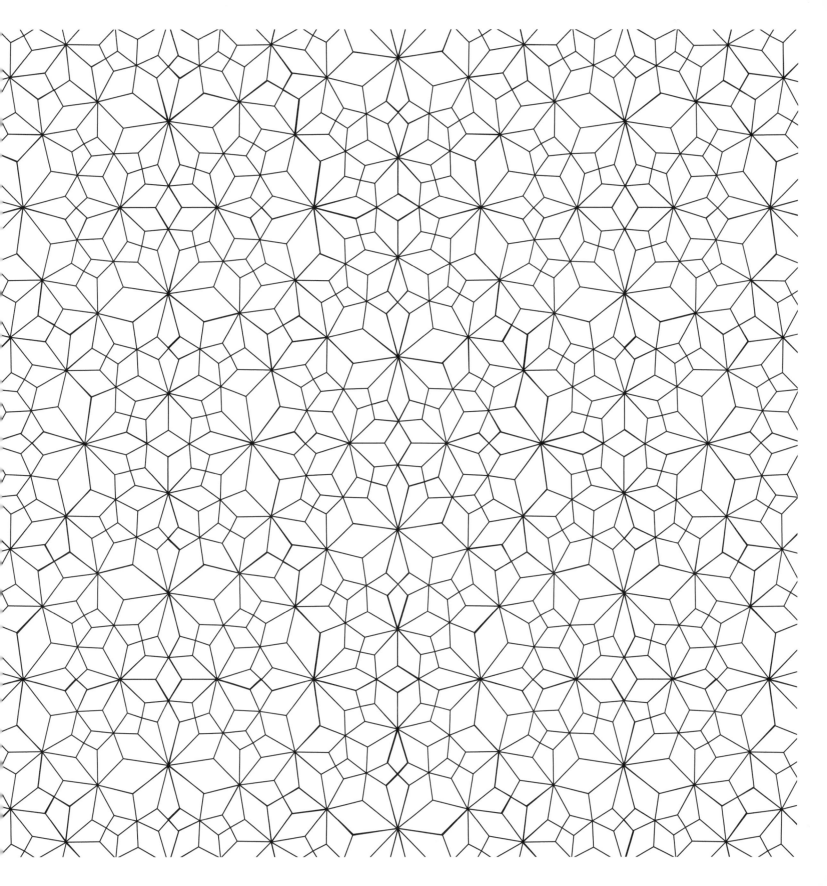

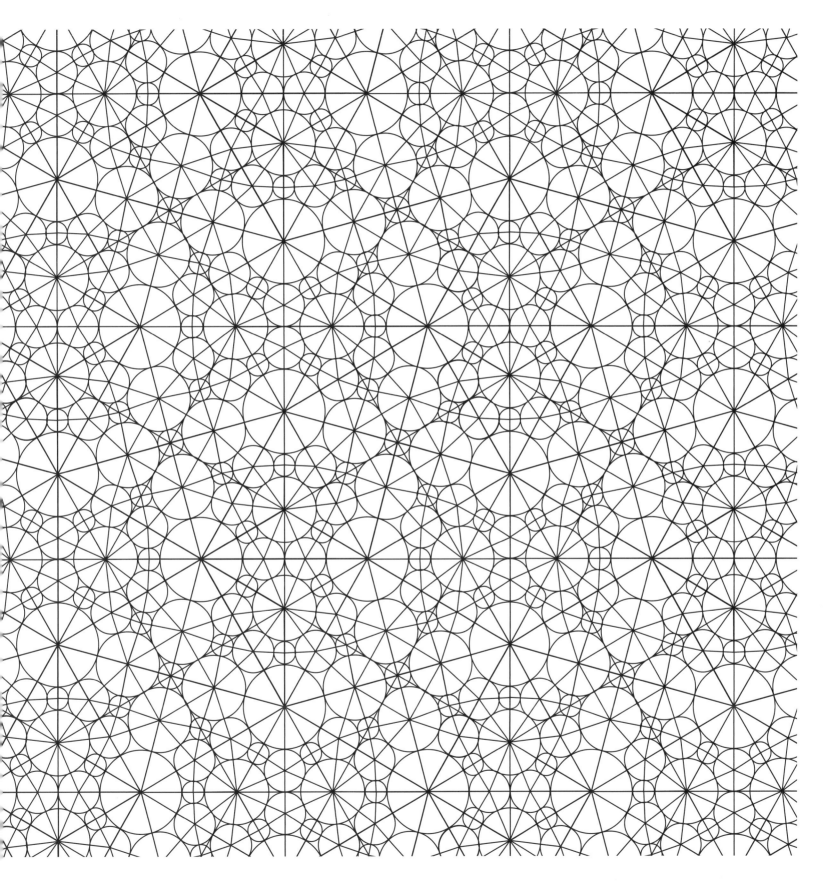

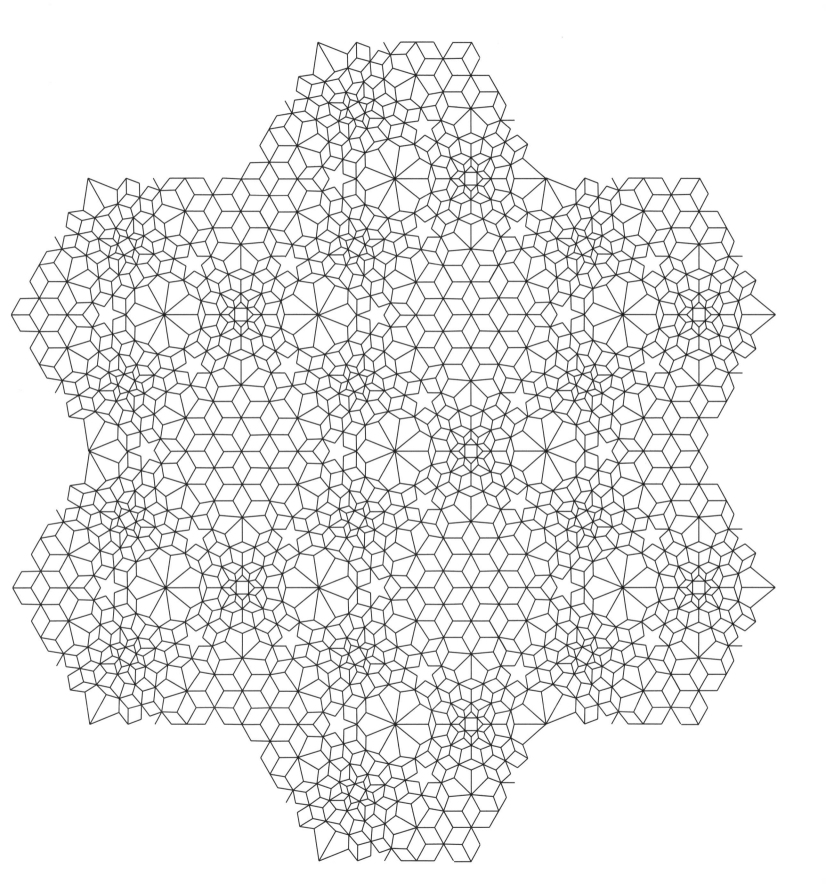

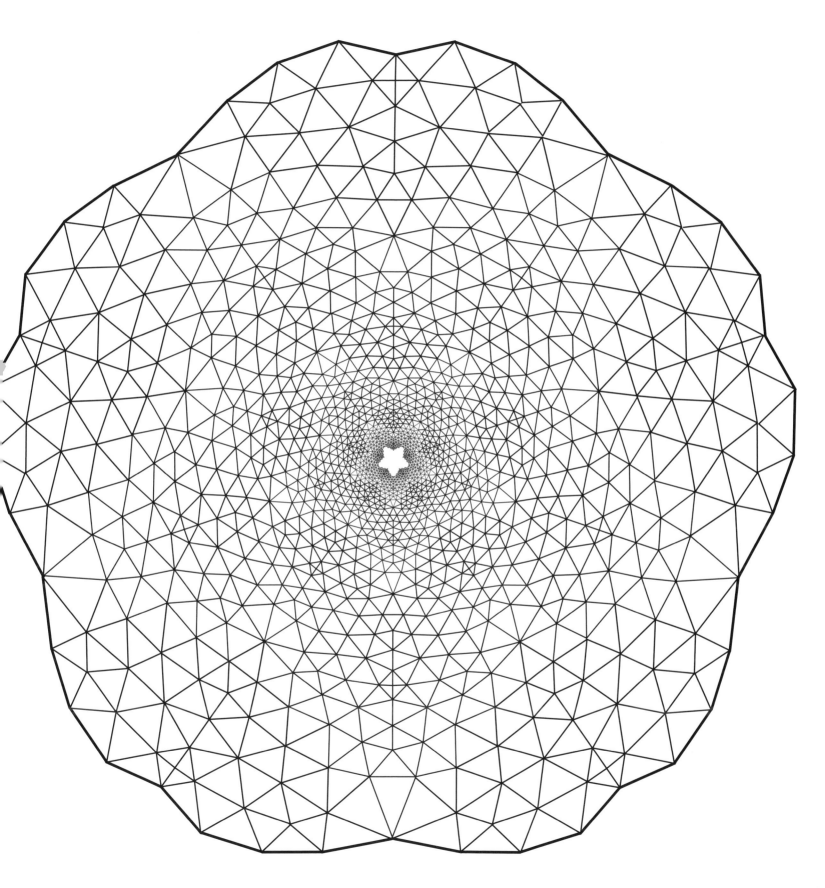

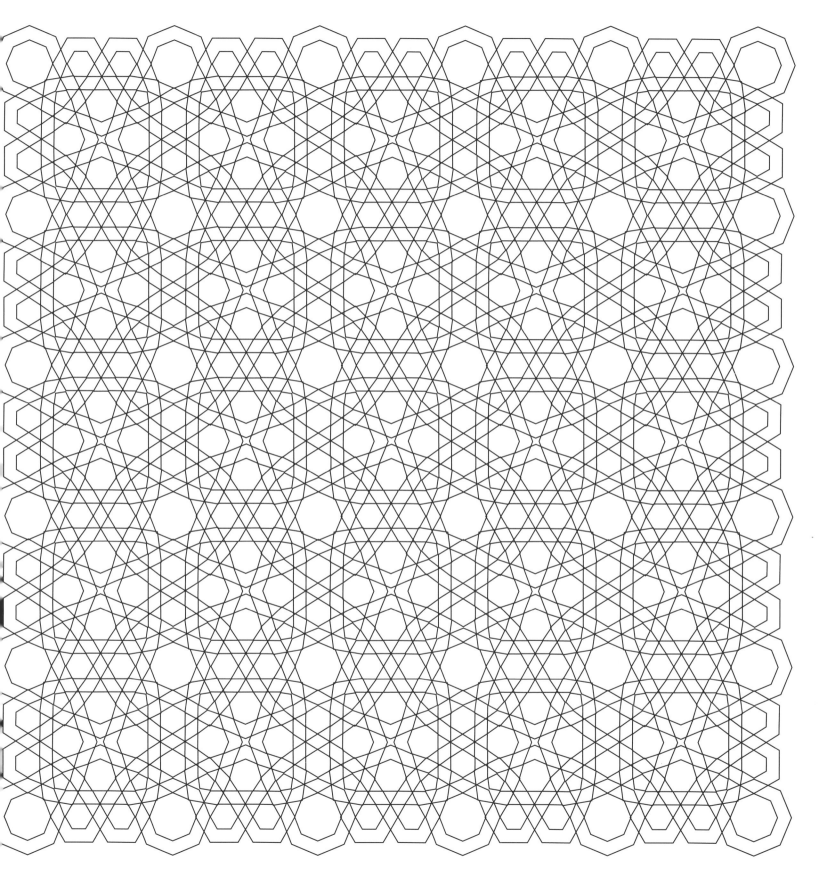

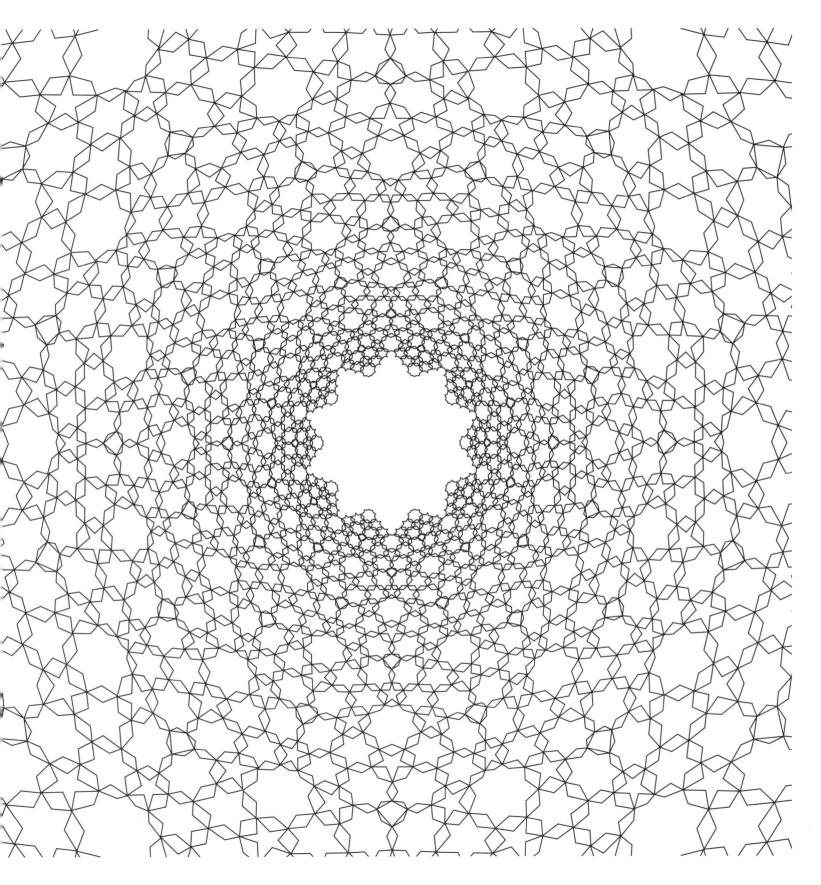

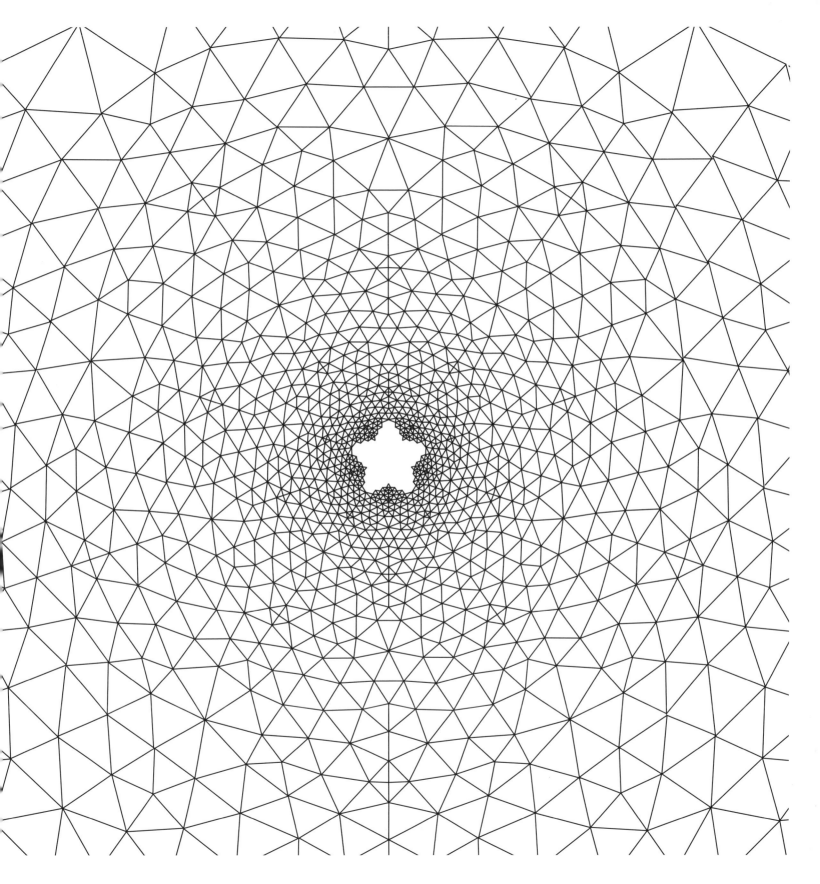

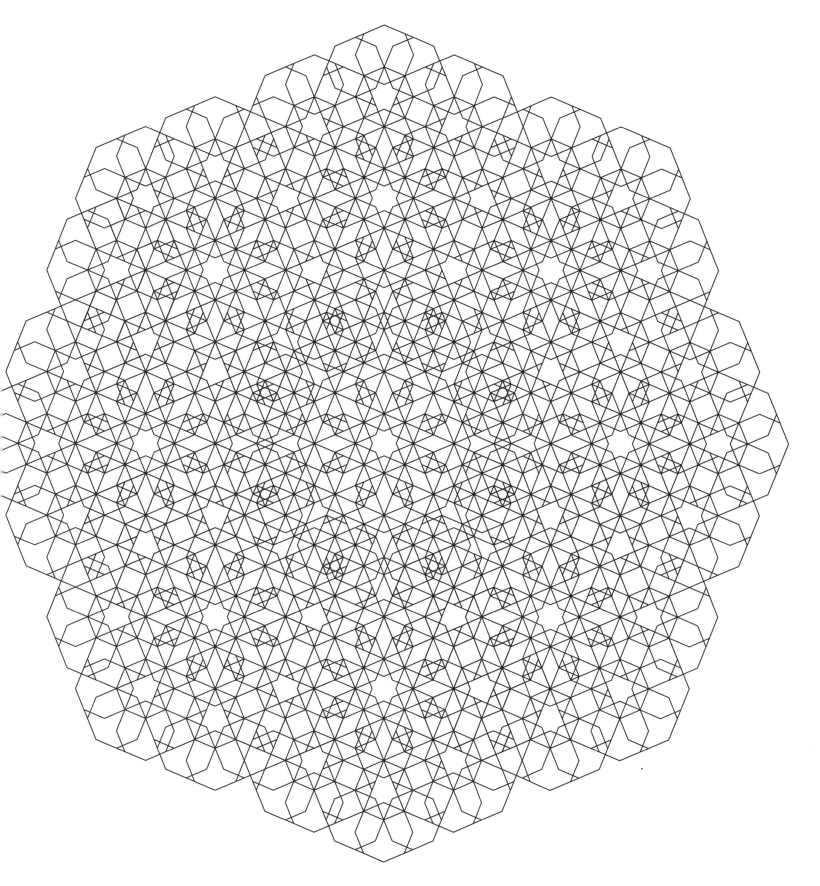

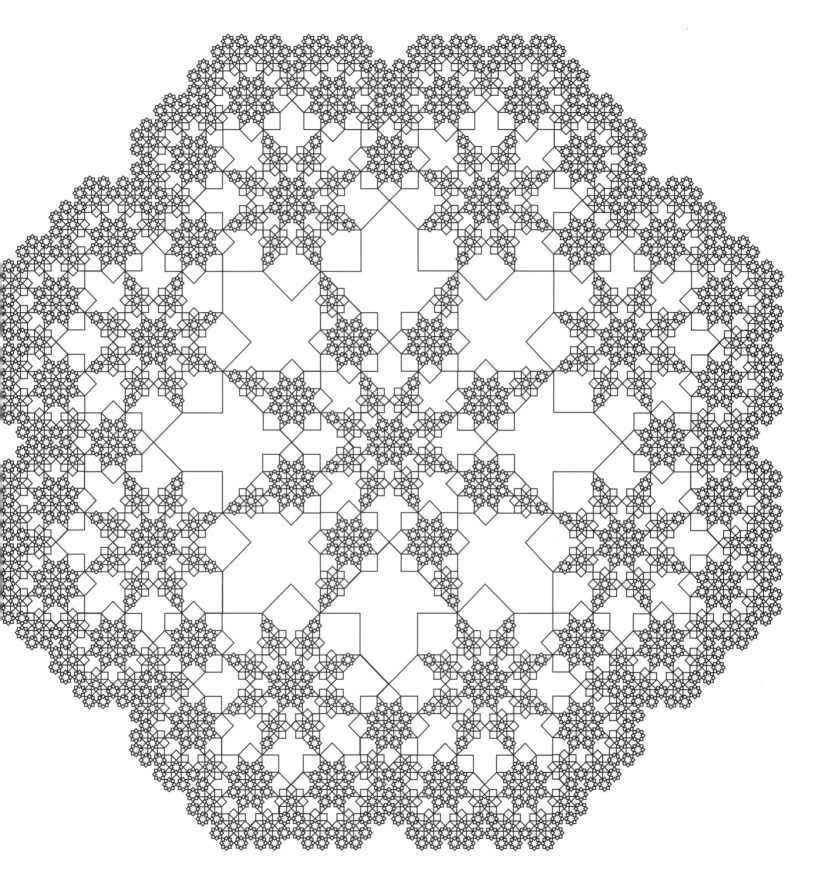

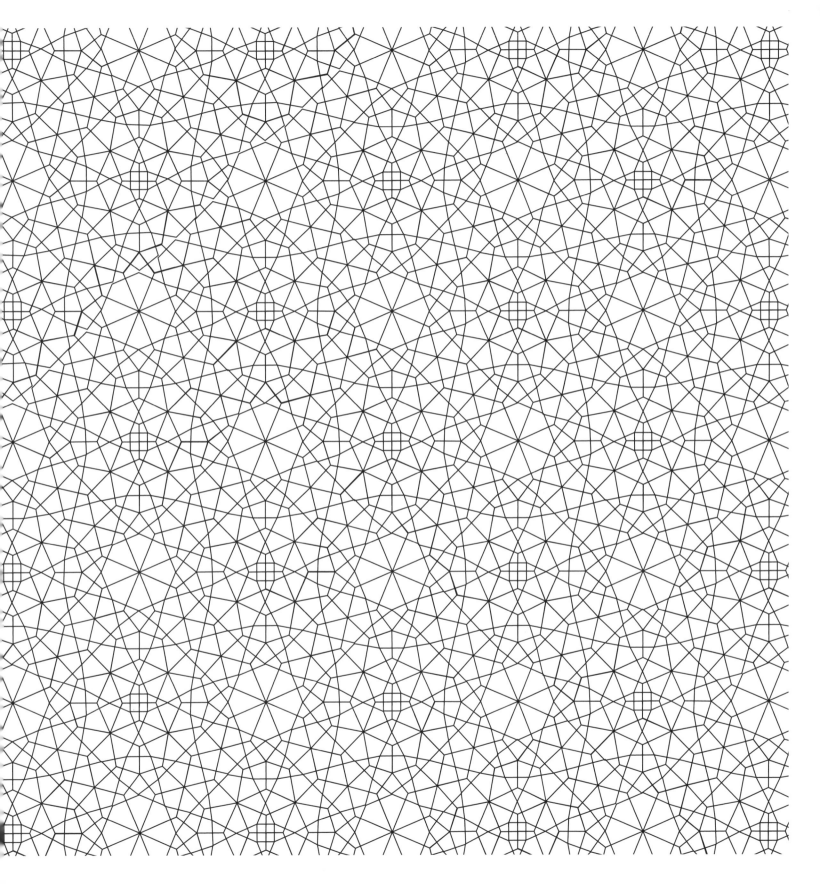

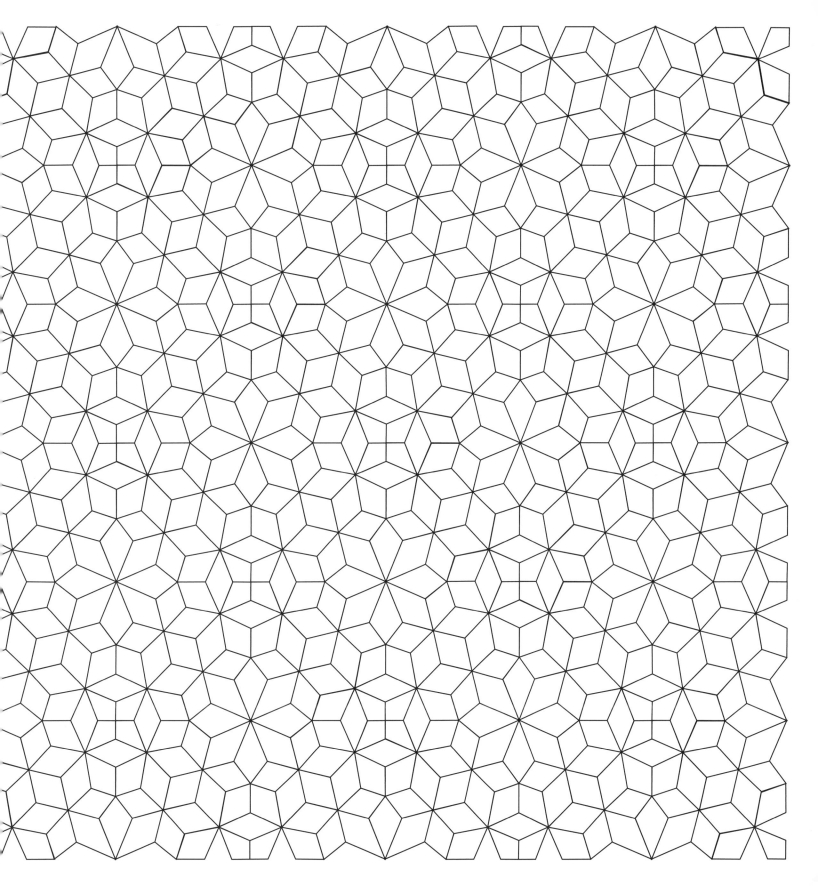

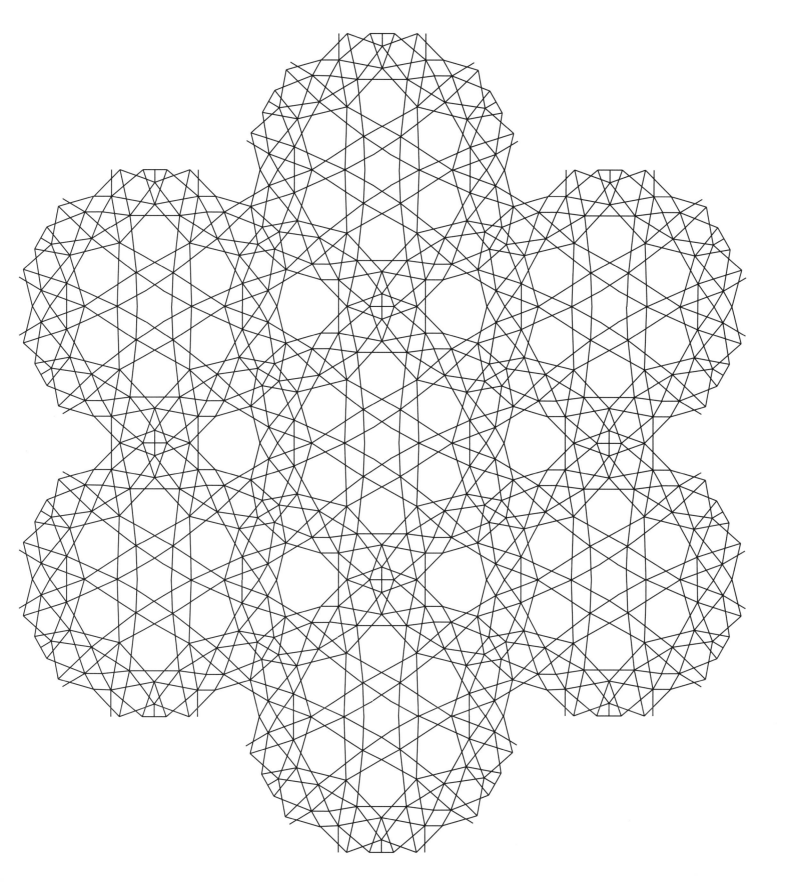

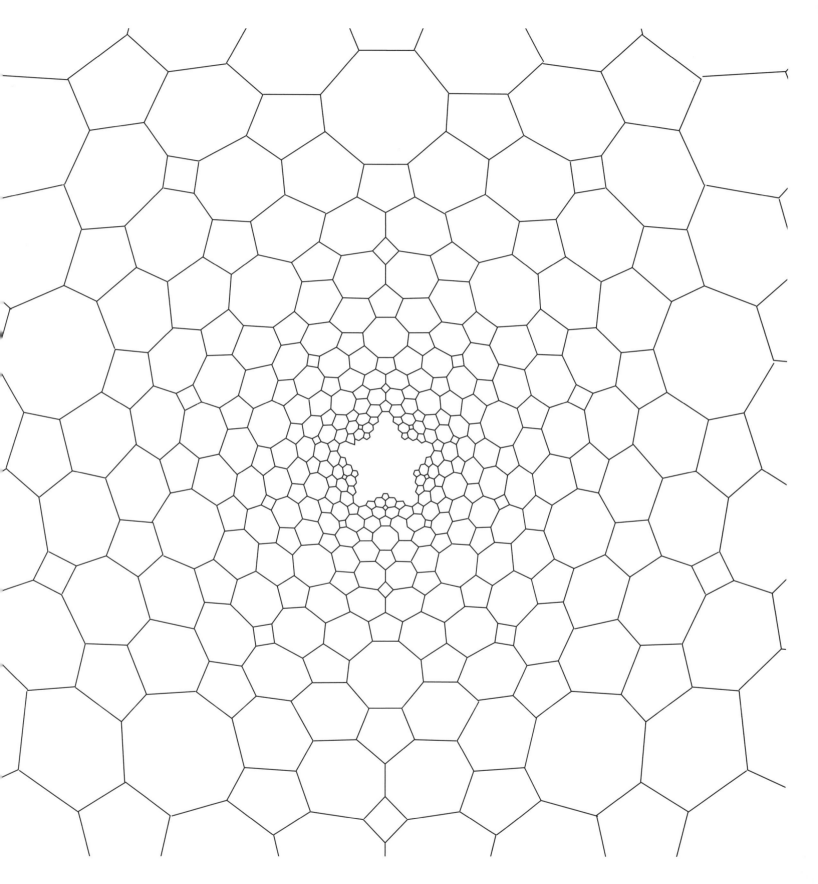

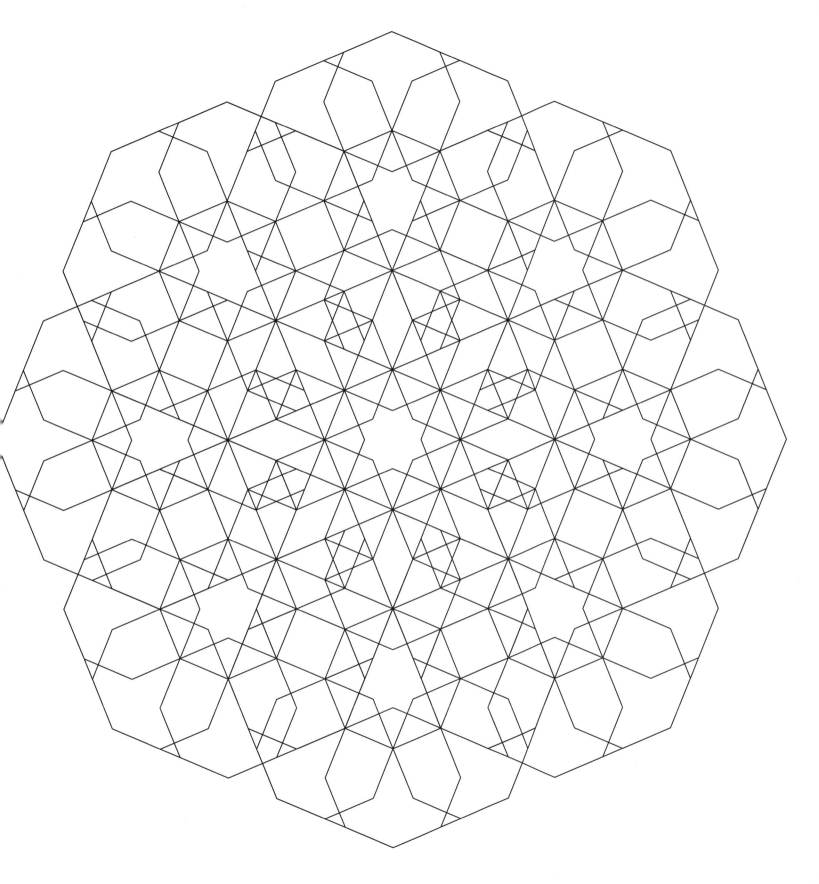

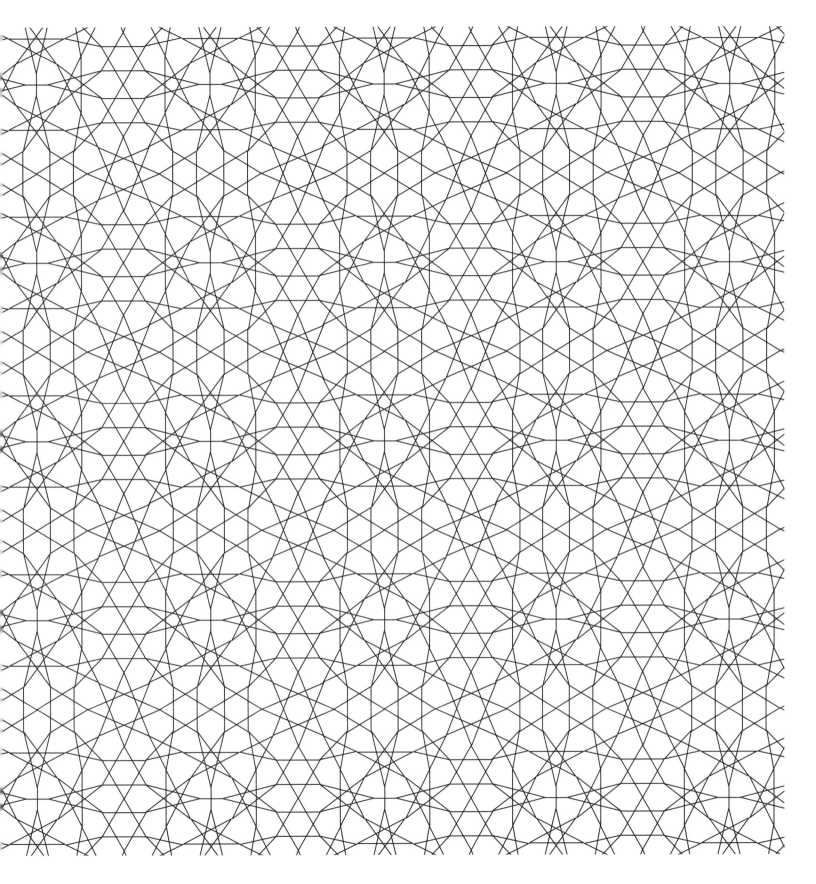

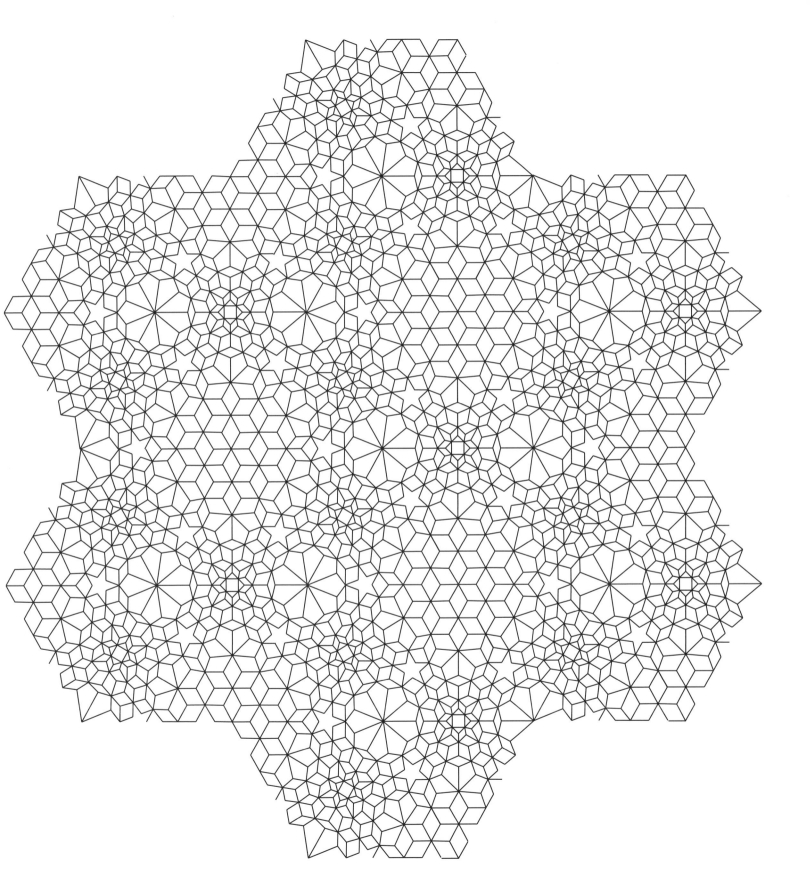

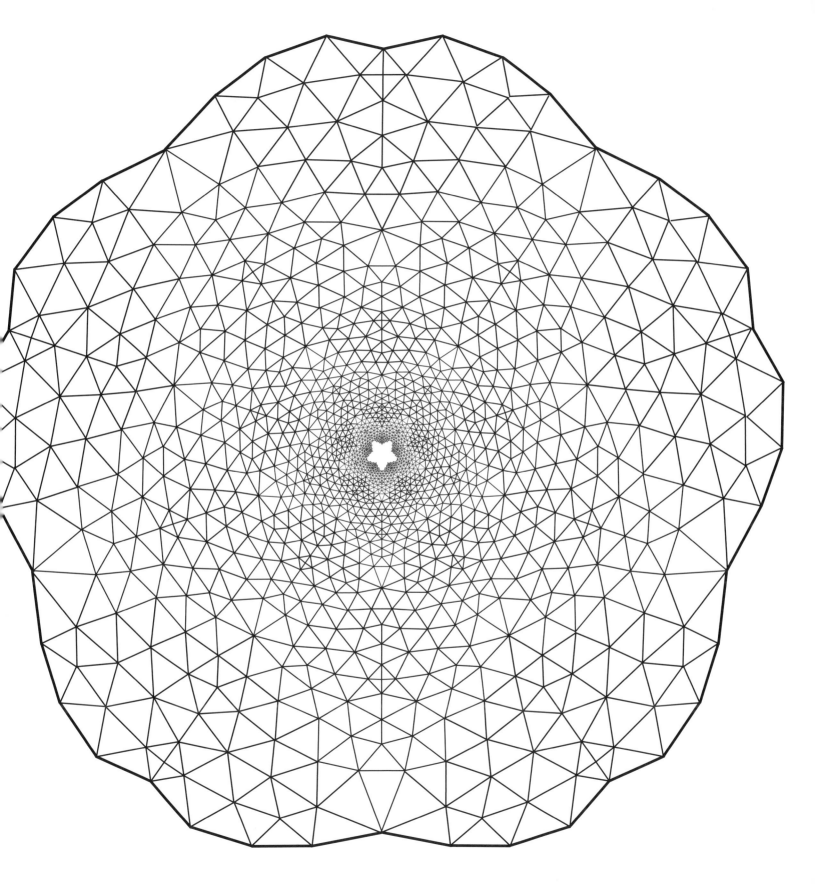

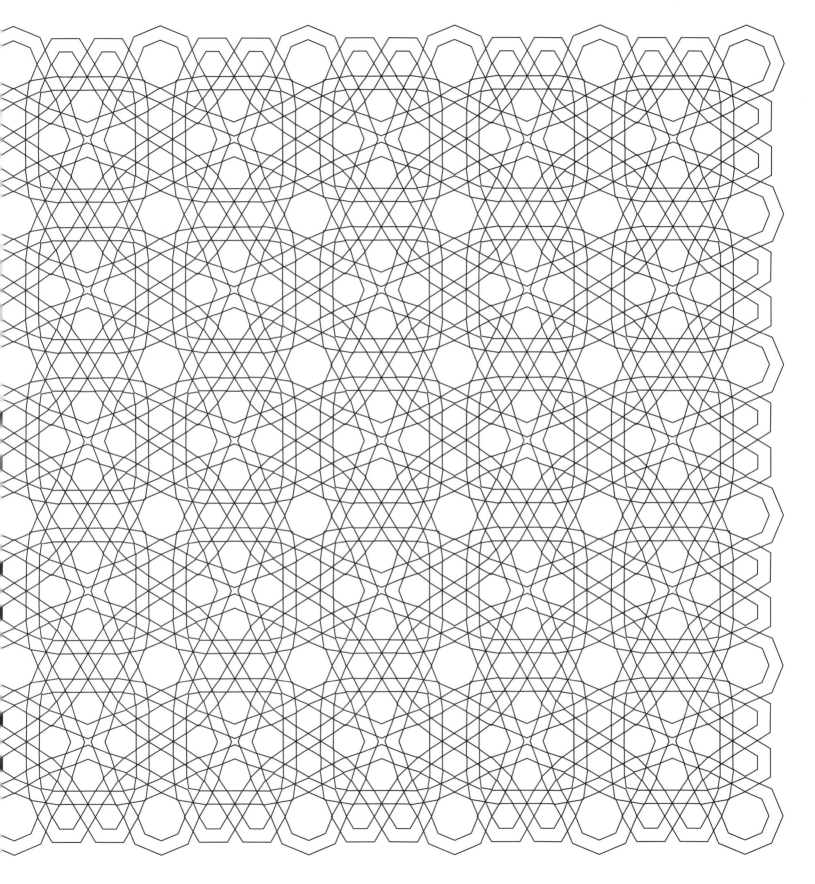

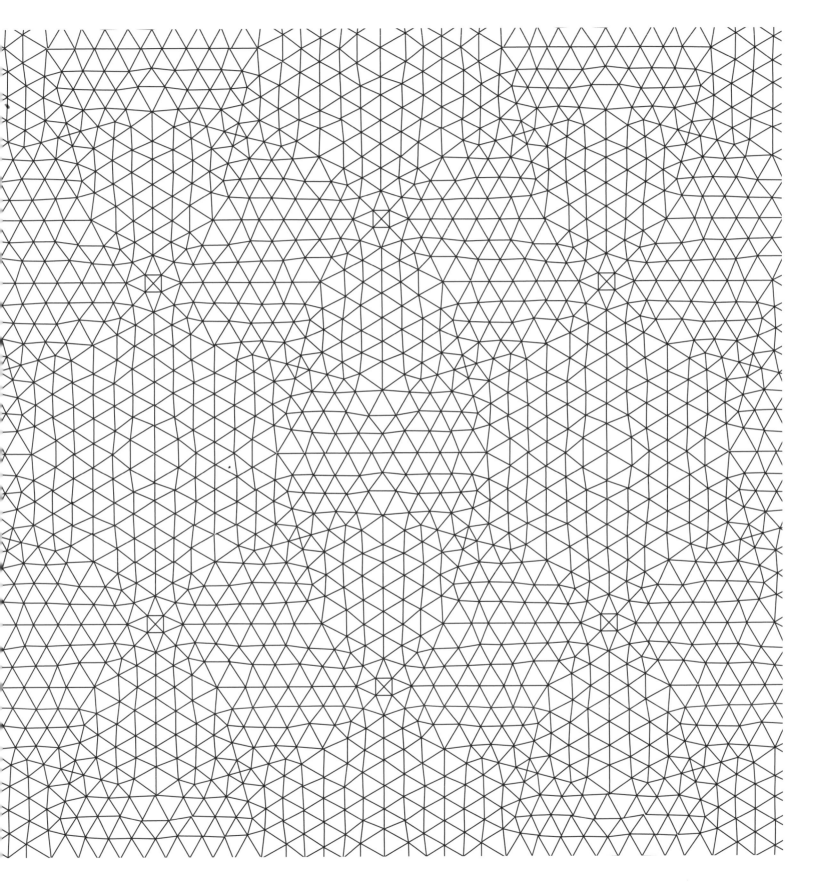

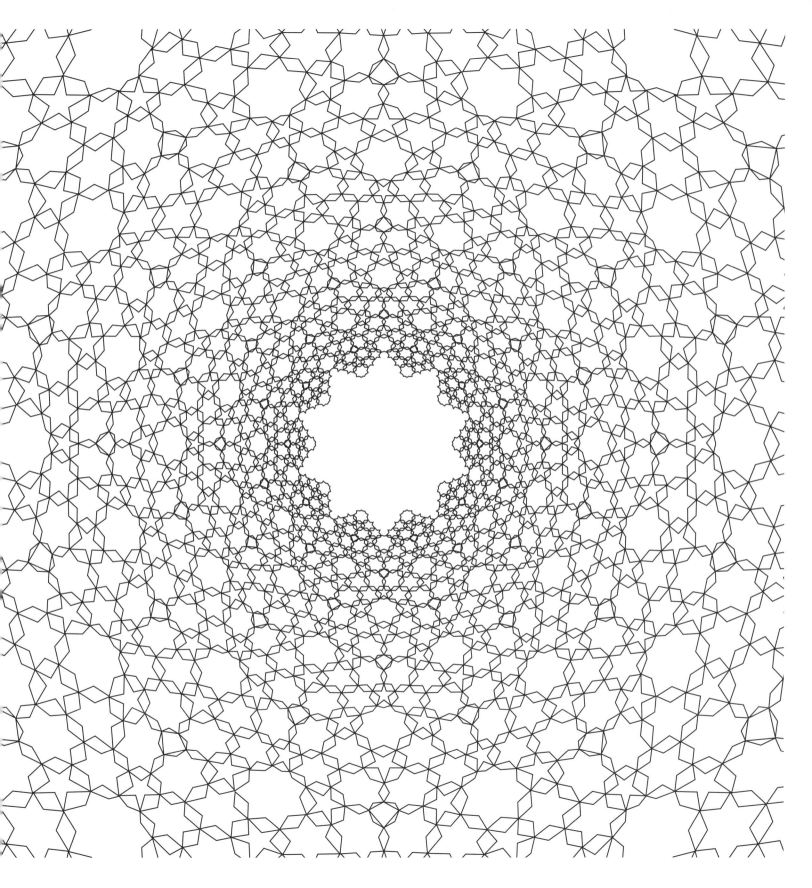

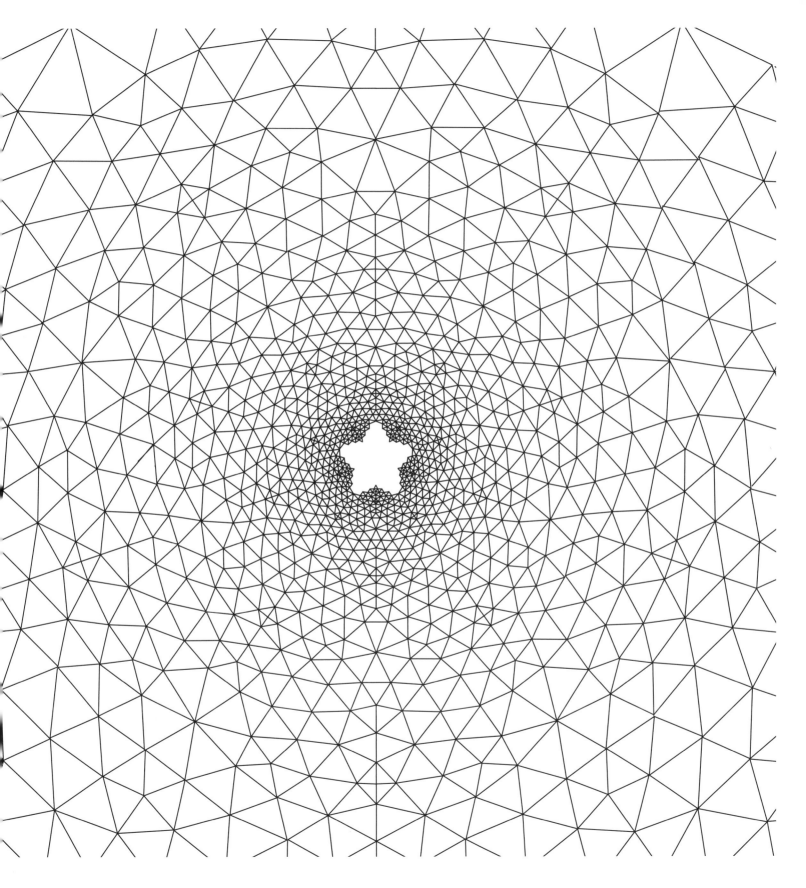

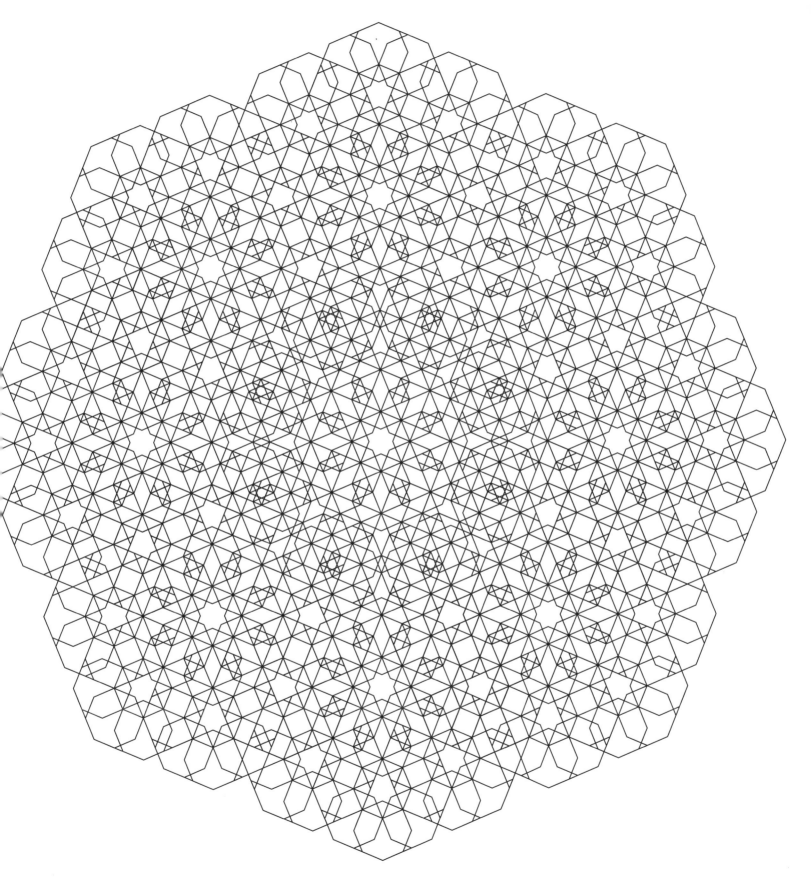

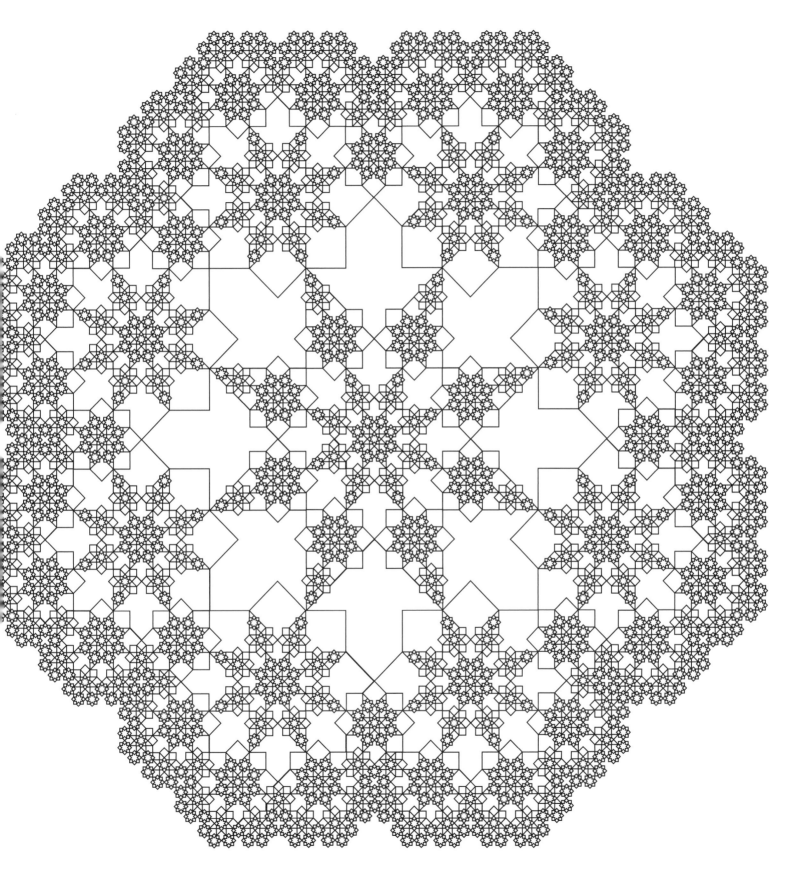

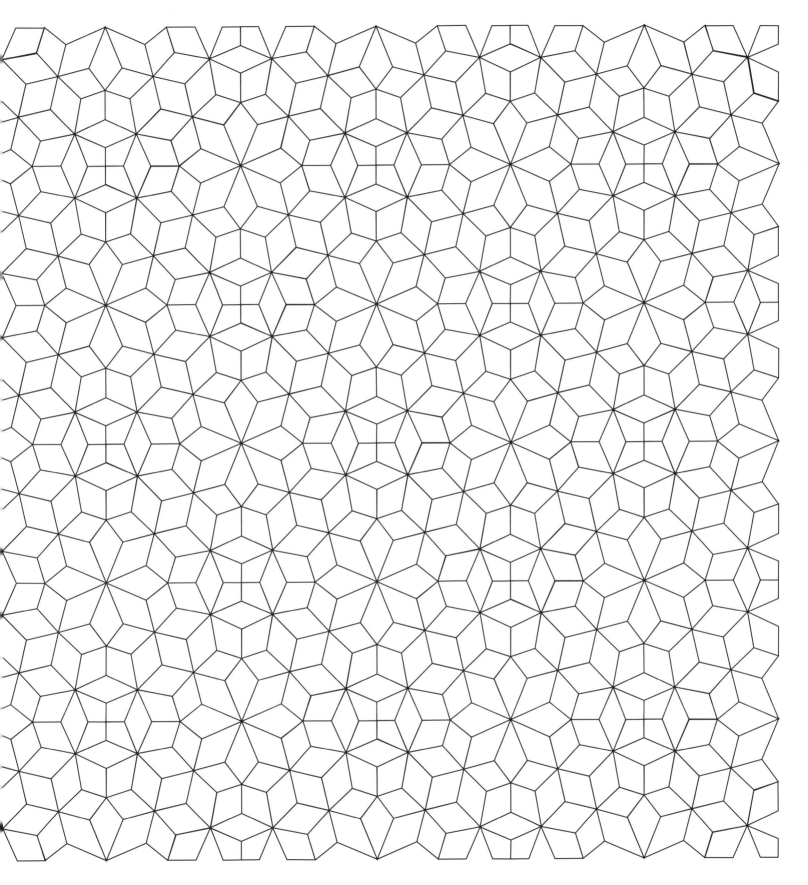

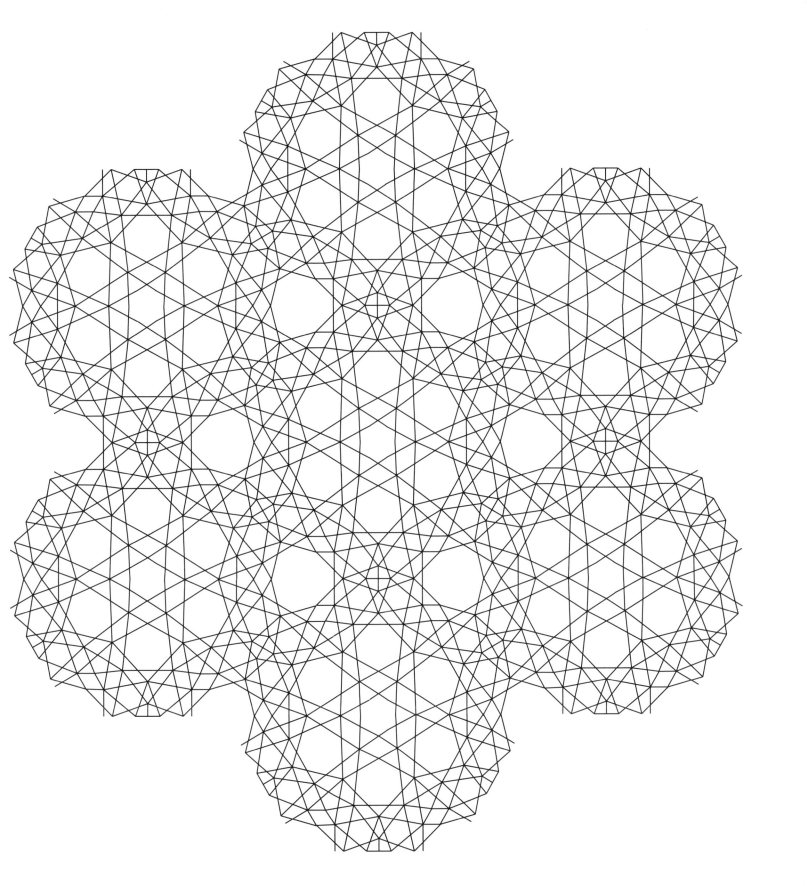

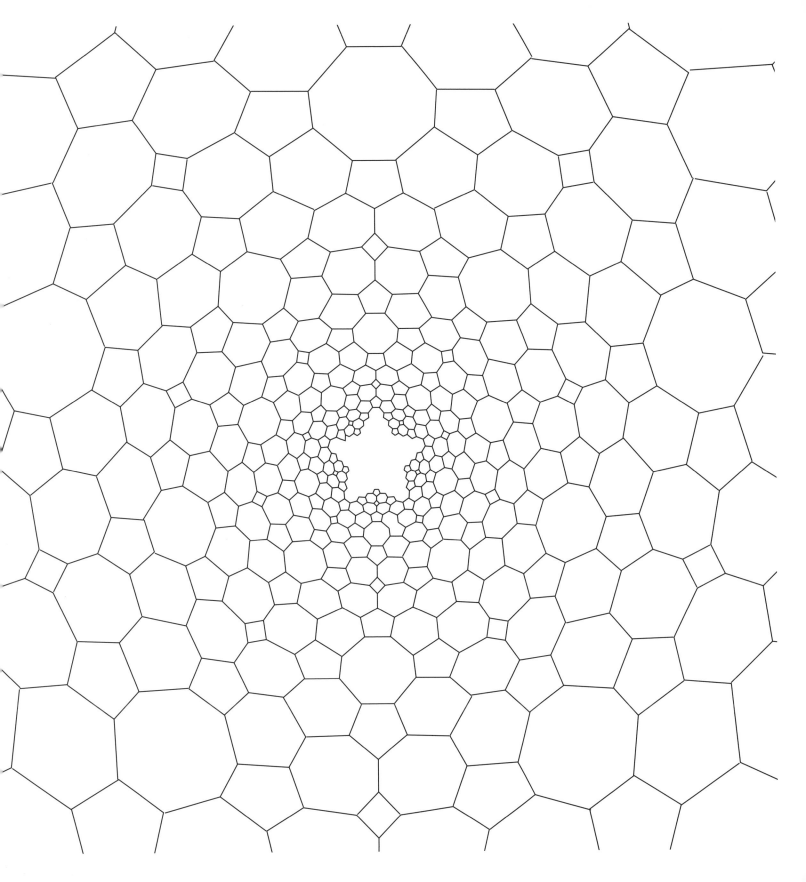

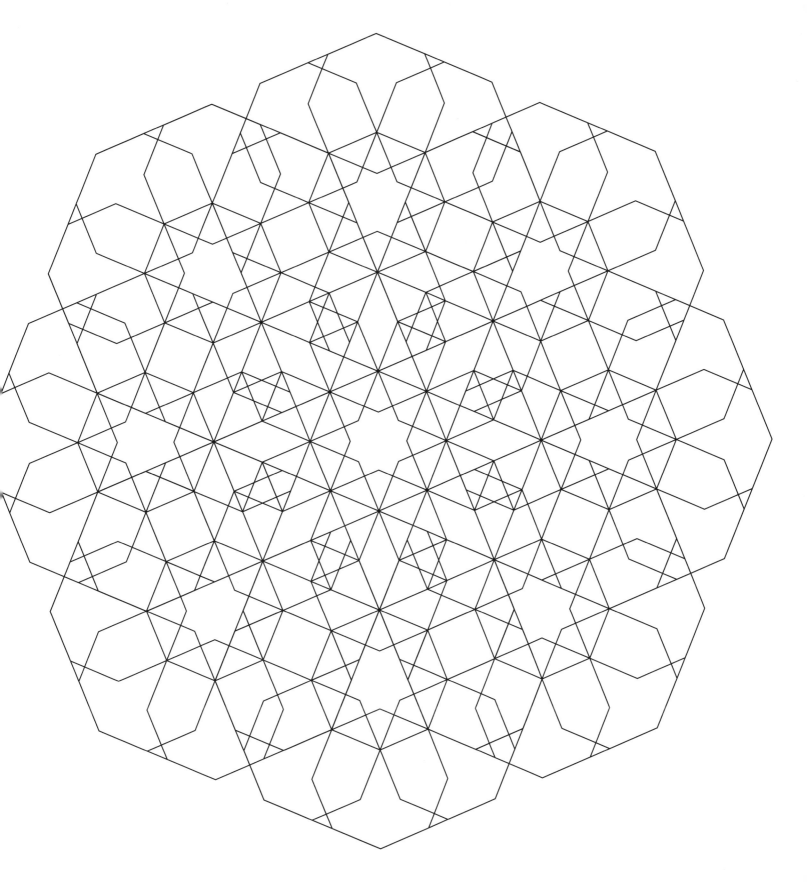